POSTCARDS HOME

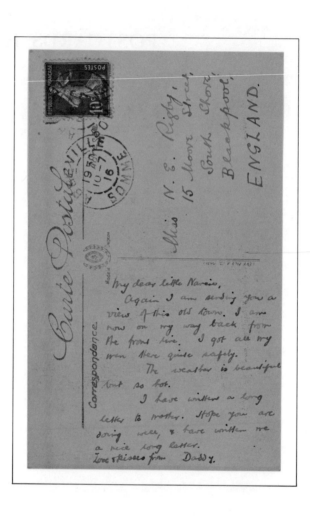

Carte Postale

Correspondence

Miss N. E. Rigby,
15 Moore Street,
South Shore,
Blackpool,
ENGLAND.

My dear little Nancie,

Again I am sending you a view of this old town. I am now on my way back from the front line. I got all my men there quite safely.

The weather is beautiful but so hot.

I have written a long letter to mother. Hope you are doing well, & have written me a nice long letter.

Love & kisses from Daddy.

POSTCARDS
HOME

Poems New and Selected

CHRISTOPHER WISEMAN

1988
Sono Nis Press
VICTORIA, BRITISH COLUMBIA

Copyright © 1988 by Christopher Wiseman

Canadian Cataloguing in Publication Data
    Wiseman, Christopher, 1936-
        Postcards home: new and selected poems
        ISBN 0-919203-87-6
        I. Title.
    PS8595.I84P6 1988   c811'.54   c88-091106-9
    PR9199.3.W58P6 1988

This book was published with the assistance of the
Canada Council Block Grant Program.

Published by
SONO NIS PRESS
1745 Blanshard Street
Victoria, British Columbia
Canada v8w 2j8

Designed, printed and bound in Canada by
MORRISS PRINTING COMPANY LTD.
Victoria, British Columbia

Acknowledgements

Some of the previously uncollected poems have appeared in the
following: *Arc, Blue Buffalo, CBC Alberta Anthology, Canadian
Literature, Canadian Writing in 1984* (U.B.C. Press), *Closings*
(Priapus Press), *CV/II, Dandelion, Encounter, Event, Grand
Piano, The New Quarterly, Ride Off Any Horison* (NeWest Press),
Translation, Whetstone, Wot.

Some poems from earlier books have subsequently appeared in the
following anthologies: *Draft* (Turnstone Press), *Hotels and Inns*
(Oxford University Press), *The Maple Laugh Forever* (Hurtig),
No Feather, No Ink (Turnstone Press), *Scroll* (Wombat Press) and
The Thomas Hardy Annual (Macmillan).

To all the editors who have printed or broadcast my poetry over
many years I would like to express my gratitude.

I would like to thank the Alberta Foundation for the Literary Arts,
Alberta Culture, The Leighton Artist Colony, the Saskatchewan
Writers' Guild, The University of Calgary, Jack and Joan Clark,
and, of course, my family, for providing me with financial support
and/or the space and time to write many of these poems.

My gratitude also goes to Mrs. Joyce Kee for all the work she has
done so cheerfully in helping to prepare the manuscript, and to
Robin Skelton for his shrewd and sympathetic editing.

In particular I want to thank Don Coles for his advice and unfailing
encouragement when I was working on this book.

Also by Christopher Wiseman

POETRY BOOKS
Waiting for the Barbarians
The Barbarian File
The Upper Hand
An Ocean of Whispers

CHAPBOOKS
Depth of Meaning
Seven Love Poems
Closings

LITERARY CRITICISM
Beyond the Labyrinth: A Study of Edwin Muir's Poetry

THIS BOOK IS FOR
THE THREE TO WHOM I SEND THE POSTCARDS HOME
Jean, Stephen, Jonathan

Memory is the sense of loss, and loss pulls us after it.
— MARILYNNE ROBINSON

Contents

*Previously
Uncollected
Poems*

MRS. ROWLEY

for Don Coles

The old gas bag, we called her. Came on Thursday
Mornings, fat and panting, to the back door,
Ten-thirty to the minute, smiling, eyes
Enormous behind her glasses, hair askew,

And sat at the kitchen table, catching her breath.
Mrs. Rowley from the grocer's shop,
Taking orders from her regulars,
But really out to talk, to share the news.

Took out her black book, fussing for it
In her bag, chatted for twenty minutes
Until, on some unknown cue, she'd lick the purple
Indelible pencil and slowly get to work.

Same as last week for the tinned fruit, is it,
Dear? We've got a new line of puddings in
And I thought of you . . . All done, she heaved
Her bulk upward, stumped down the back steps

And wheezed happily away, losing herself
In the long streets like a soft giant ghost.
Mrs. Rowley, gas bag, figure of fun
In a child's world, back to her corner shop,

To custard-powder, potted meat and spices.
The next morning, a huge brown box of food
Would somehow appear at our door, as if from on high,
Fragrant, packed lovingly. Those fat fingers!

Until she stopped coming. One day she just stopped.
Big, gossiping, slow-walking Mrs. Rowley
Came no more to talk, to make the food
Appear without a sound on our white scrubbed steps.

Mrs. Rowley, the gas bag, up, up, and up,
Up over the city, high and away, out
Of our lives, past new dark clouds coming in;
Mrs. Rowley sailing, towing her time

Behind her, wheezing not at all as she soared,
Pulling away a world of gentleness,
A world of slowness and great courtesy,
A world where words were spoken and food was there.

IN THE BANFF SPRINGS HOTEL

Their furniture is still here —
The dusty high-backed chairs, old
Mahogany desks for letters home,
Brocade covers, velvet curtains —

And it is easy to see them sitting,
Horses stabled by willing grooms,
Mountain clothes unpacked, laid out,
Ready for a bracing promenade,

Or with plummy voices ordering
Pink gins before dinner, maids
Wisping past in black dresses
And starched aprons, waiters gliding,

Deferential, well-tipped, in awe
Of such intrepid wanderers
Of Empire revelling in their history.
What tales to tell of mountains and bears!

And it's still their place. Their ghosts
Sit with rugs over their knees
Looking up the valley. The red
Of the map brought them all this way

To take the healing waters, or see
The real sublime before they died.
Some came to find needed remoteness
Or ease creaking bones. No matter why.

To dream of building this out here,
So far from anything, and then
Transform it into magnificence,
Shows they were special in their way,

That it's too easy to dismiss them,
Those parodies with white moustaches,
Pale ladies in silk and muslin, butlers,
Maids, world-labelled steamer-trunks,

Their tough proud ridiculousness.
Today diminishment — loud kids,
Jeans, cheap trinkets, banks of video-games —
And I surprise an anger in myself,

A fierce desire for stylishness,
And I feel, from the wide terraces,
From card-tables and smoking-rooms,
Flushed, braying, their ghosts approve.

THE BELL

for Dennis Hamley

It's had a facelift to cater to the times.
The dirty wooden furniture is gone,
The walls parade new fashionable colours,

There's soup and quiche and home-made shepherd's pie
At the bar, the old toilets in the cobbled yard,
Reeking of piss and puke, carbolic and worse,

Have been replaced by clean sweet rooms inside.
But it can't disguise itself that easily.
In jackets and ties we eat and look around,

Our thoughts back all those years when this was the place
We came most nights, down the hill from the camp,
The place we staggered back from, singing, lurching,

Being eighteen and learning drink. Here we mixed
Rum and cider, ale and Drambuie, swapped
Dirty jokes, exaggerated our sexual

Encounters, planned glorious golden futures,
Heard each others' hopes, made quick friends
And quicker enemies. The Bell. The Bell.

Then we were never going to get old,
Put on weight, become tied down, depressed.
And now we two sit here again, quietly —

Family men, tired, hair receding —
Look round, talk of those who sat here once,
Remember all the wild and gentle ones,

Wonder about the meaning of recollection.
We toast each other as we were then, a quarter
Century ago, drinking to our lost ghosts,

Drinking goodbye to the thin young men in blue,
Goodbye, too, to The Bell, for it's doubtful we
Shall be back, drinking to this surprising meeting,

To our children, as old now as we were then.
My friend, we're middle-aged and going fast,
Far quicker than these old walls and roof

Which just need paint and care to outlast us.
We leave, not mentioning what we know, that up
The hill they've ploughed the camp six feet under.

HARVEST, 1943

Far off, lazy, autumnal,
A fading period-piece
Of a mild and bursting landscape
Is how my middle-age
Would like to remember it.
Coward memory, you lie.
You leave out the bombers
Roaring overhead, our fathers
Away, mothers crying,
A world which killed on sight.

But then only the wheatfield
Mattered to us, the lusting,
As the blades cut the square smaller
And at last the rabbits ran,
And we ran too to kill,
To kill, and kill again.
Murderous epiphany.
That day a frenzy took me
Like nothing I've known since.
Weasel memory, you bite.

There was no pity in my frantic
Child's muscles on the blood-wet
Stick crashing down and down.
No pity. No check. Just joy.
It was later, much later,
Gold help me, long after
Some of our fathers came back,
After the cities and camps were gone,
That I began to see it clearly —
That sunlit day of murder,
Children, the blood, the war,
Weapons raised,
Terrified dark eyes.

KENSINGTON GARDENS, MAY 1982

Subdued. Headlines have stared at us
All day with news of ships sunk in the South
Atlantic by sudden missiles nothing could stop.
We've come to sit, to find normality.
Shirt-sleeves. Summer dresses. Distant traffic.
Children play or are wheeled by in the sun.
Ducks lead trails of camouflaged offspring,
Seeking bread. A convoy of them glides past
When a gull appears from nowhere, huge, ugly,
Skimming the surface of the green water,
Takes the last duckling and carries it
To a flat stone in the middle of the pond
Where another waits. They hold it down and beak
Its guts and eyes through a desperate downy flutter.
A thin unbroken scream goes on and on.

Kensington Gardens. The right place for small
Contentments. Today the headlines and now this.
There's anger in me. The gulls preen on their rock,
Then one takes off again, seeking the convoys.
I leave my paper, its news of war and bodies,
Turn my back, stride quickly away, hearing
Terrible wings, fast wings over water.

THE FLY

Tired, I reach into the bookshelf.
It must have been before the war
That this one was last opened
And there's a fly pressed into a page
Like a blemish in the paper.

My father's book, bought and read
The year of my birth,
The inscription and date there.
This fly's death is as old as I am.

And I think of how it might have been.
From family photographs
I imagine that the fly belonged
To a Yorkshire garden perpetually in sun,
The book to a thin young man
With a pipe and baggy trousers,
And he to a woman with funny hats

Always tending a teapot on the grass.
The camera lies. Patterns don't exist
The way we want them to.
But it's not hard to see
In this pathetic dried corpse
Long years of decline and falling away,
A generation reading in deckchairs,
While somewhere else, a long way off,
A poisoned Europe swelled to bursting.

I look at it,
Willing the legs to twitch,
The wings to start a slow soft beat,
For I would have it move and soar,
Would have it escape the book,
Fly free out of my mind for ever.

I would bring back all the war-dead,
More than fifty million since this book was closed,
To sit innocent again in sunshine,
Taking photographs and reading books
Under the friendly drone of flies.

POSTCARDS HOME

I hold them. Two cards so well preserved
That except for slightly faded ink and sepia
Photographs they could have been written
Last year. Both show Abbeville, the first
Franked Army Post Office, 7 July 1916;
The other, three days later, simply The Somme,
As if it were some holiday resort.
The first seems hurried, nervous.

*This is a fine cathedral which you can see
in the distance. The streets are just as narrow
as they look. Dy.*

          The second different,
More relaxed.

*   My dear little Nancie,
again I am sending you a view of this old town.
I am now on my way back from the front
line. I got all my men there quite safely.
The weather is beautiful but so hot. I have
written a long letter to mother. Hope
you are doing well and have written me a nice
long letter. Love and kisses from Daddy.*

Grandfather, I never knew you. You died early.
I think you could have taught me, steadied me.
God knows what you described in that long letter.
I read the cards again, that calm unshaken
Handwriting (for all you knew your final words)
And I wonder what they felt when these came
Through the door. A simple soaring excitement
For the girl, remembered from so far away,
So strong she kept them for sixty-five years.
For the woman a great rinse of relief from nightmares
Of mortars and barbed-wire, from the immense terrors.
Tears in her room, perhaps, cleaning, then
A letter back.

        Such an ordinary address —
15 Moore Street, South Shore, Blackpool, England.

ONE FOR THE BODY

The shell exploded so close
That you were hurled against the side of the trench
And your back was smashed.
Stretcher, ambulance, train, hospital —
You were lucky, I suppose.

Today I hold your identification discs,
Hard pressed cardboard, one grey and one brown,
Joined now by a piece of household string,
Kept all these years by your daughter.
Now seventy-six, she is tidying her life
And wanted me to have them.

Hard to think that these were in that trench,
Round your neck through all that mud and dying,
Next to your skin under the rough serge
In the cold sweat of fear and pain.
Too intimate. Yet I want them. I have nothing
Else of you, grandfather, except a few photographs
And two postcards you sent to my aunt
From the Somme. We never met. You died. I was born.
So I keep them and shall hand them on
To my sons, knowing that to hold them
Is to unlock something in a family line,
Give substance to time. A strange meeting, this,
For they bring me closer to myself, make one man,
An unknown ancestor, seem real, make a heart
Open out which was closed to you before.

Two discs. One for the body,
One for official records and the death letter home.
The string holding them is strong.

THE BIRDWATCHER   *for Don McKay*

Knowing I was desperate to see a goldfinch,
And shocked at my robbing nests for eggs,
My mother talked to me, gave me a notebook
And pencil, and told me to go up on the Knox
And, like grown-ups, record the birds I saw.
She said she thought there were goldfinches
Up there in the gorse and thistles.
So I went, found a hiding place, started
Making notes in the wartime sun.
There was nothing much to see — some skylarks,
Pigeons, chaffinches — and I was bored.
I daydreamed goldfinches and eggs I would swap
When suddenly I heard it, a new noise,
Low and loud, heading straight towards me,
And then, right over my head, scattering birds,
Deafening, rocketing from behind the hill,
Came my first Mustang, about a hundred
Feet up, enormous for a fighter, air-scoop,
Squared wings, American squadron markings.
Pulse thumping, head singing, mad with joy,
I stood and saw it dive down to the sea,
Make a snappy climbing turn, and streak
Away down the coast towards Filey.
I wrote in my new notebook, very big,
First Mustang sighted. Scarborough, 1944.
The way it ripped the air! Its suddenness!
And I stopped stealing eggs then, gave my
Collection away to surprised friends,
Forgot the goldfinch I had never seen.

Later I filled that book with other things —
A V-1 Flying Bomb, off course, right over
The Knox, exotic Lockheed Lightnings,
Thunderbolts, Typhoons, new marks of Spitfire —
But nothing could compare with that first Mustang,
That huge shape roaring above me the day
I went looking for a goldfinch. From then on
The wild wings were in me, a magic bird
Big as imagination, which down inside
I carry even now.

NEEDS

Beacon Hill Park, early March, after rain,
And I'm straight from the white death-house of the prairies.

I'm not much interested in the lakes and trees,
The peacocks parading like bad motel paintings,

The world's tallest and dullest totem-pole,
Or even the mild green giving of grass under my shoes.

Today it's the crocuses that I am stopped by,
The astounding fields of them, white and blue,

Reaching upward, opening to the weather,
A fury in them as if they would be taller,

As if they would defy whatever it is
Decrees they must not grow too much, turn giants,

As if they were desperate to go all the way,
If they were allowed, up into cloud and beyond.

I go on, down to the beach, smelling secrets
Of my childhood in the salt of a freshening wind,

Down to the sandhoppers and shining driftwood,
Sea-bleached, eaten hollow, heaped at random

Like a bone-house for enormous frozen beasts.
I balance on a huge white spine of log,

Looking past the birds into the horizon,
My mind dizzy, white and blue with distance,

And I raise my frozen hands. I would be taller.
I feel the fury in me. Today I would

Go all the way, no holding back. I reach
And, look, already the clouds are higher, lifting.

THE PROFESSOR DANCES TO ELVIS   *for J.H.*

Eight months since they removed the disc
And after all the pain I didn't trust it,
Couldn't believe it would ever be right again,
But before I sensed such sudden conspiracy
You had my hand, pulling me to the dance-floor,
Friends laughing and cheering, and I was dancing,
Dancing, just swaying at first, but not hurting,
And soon I tried more, moving stronger, faster,
Even twisting myself a bit, and I knew,
Right then, that I'd be better, it had worked.
Then suddenly your request (I found out later)
For Elvis was coming hard at me, wonderfully hard —
All Shook Up — and I was throwing myself about,
Pouring sweat, grinning, free again, free
After years. Then, softly, the low young voice,
And we're holding on, slow dancing, my hand
Soaking the back of your purple dress, my brow
Dripping into your hair, our hands holding slippery —
Love me tender, love me sweet, never let me go —
And the room was nearly gone, it was time travel,
And I was there but back too at those first dances,
Sailing thirty years to meet new feelings,
Then back again, eyes closed, your thighs
A slither of nylon under the thin dress,
Riding my legs, me floating and swaying —
Love me tender, love me true, all my dreams fulfill —

Where have those first girls gone, but now
Just sweat and sway and rhythm and Elvis and you
And no pain, no pain at all, just remembered things
Repossessing me — *Love me tender, love me long* —
And we danced the room into oblivion, and you
Had cured me, killed the demons, and I thought
How just weeks before you were a serious student
Sitting quietly at my seminar table, so
Impossibly far from this soft wet dancing,
From your giving me my old body back,
From you and Elvis flying me away.

ABUNDANCES   *for Jim Crenner*

(Compelled,
I pick up my pen to write to you.)
Red with sunburn I sit in a cedar
House by a mountain lake,
Shaking off suburbs. (The accumulation
Has me stunned; you know I'm not
A nature poet, a birdwatcher.)
A meadowlark on a power-pole has sung
The same seven notes for four hours
(A bit like an Adderly phrase
On that record we used to listen to.)
A woodpecker lays down a beat.
Swallows swerve round the eaves,
Nests full of gaping frenzy, coming
Back over and over, their lives
One purpose (I think of people
I have known, special people —
The self-sacrifice, the nurturing
To the point of exhaustion.)
Accumulations, I said. Birds.
A yellow one fast at ground level,
Blue ones on a fence, a kestrel
Hovering, precise and delicate,
A speckled one swinging on a grass,
Different kinds of ducks on the lake,
A great blue heron trailing
Huge across the surface. (You
Should have seen it — those slow
Wings, the arrogance of size!)
Last night, dark, a big owl
Just over my head, the air
Whistling softly in its glide.

I wait for eagle, osprey, kingfisher,
(I'm getting greedy but everything
Else seems to have come to me.)
There are humming-birds, a manic loon,
Blackbirds, robins, big hawks.
(Old friend, with your binoculars
And books you'd know more
Of this than I, but I feel
Strangely favoured. You go looking.
I just sit quietly and hear
My blood jumping again.)
Insects everywhere, great trout
Splashing blue and silver
In the black water, miles of trees
Marching up mountains
And higher there's still deep snow,
Even in July, even in this heat.
(We should be sharing this. We
Should be sharing it, my pen writes.)
At night the coyotes, high and clear,
Their song bouncing off hills.
The Northern Lights — benevolent
Cataclysm — seeming to reach
A silent grace towards me
In the smell of pine and cedar.
(Yes, I am enfolded, and I just
Wanted to tell you about it.
You will understand when I say
That such abundances are blessings.
You will not begrudge me
When I feel things touch my lips
Soft as a kiss when I sleep.)

DEAD ANGELS

No more dancing on heads of pins
Or sunning themselves on sunlit clouds.
No more celestial music in our dreams,
Bending near the earth with harps of gold,
Standing high with trumpets over congregations.
And something else will have to be assigned
To be the guardian of children's souls
And give protection from nightmares or hunger.

For these are dead angels I look at
In a monastery storeroom, where a key
And curiosity have led me. Half-dark,
The air hot and thick, blinds drawn on the sun,
Here, among assorted relics of the years,
Among fly corpses and damaged furniture,
Are four angels in a corner, line astern,
Tilted awkwardly together in the silence.

I'm not surprised the monks didn't smash them.
I couldn't. It would be desecration,
Seeing the blue robes, the Victorian doll
Faces, the white and pink and gold,
The long feathered wings furled right down
Their backs. But see the thick dust coating
The bright blue eyes and caught in the folds
Of feathers. A shock. There's been a great fall here.

These presences should never turn to dust,
Nor be piled up, grounded, silenced, abandoned
In such a place. What monstrous innodation!
Compelled, I move around. In the shadows
The wings are deformities, turning them
Suddenly into cruel ugly three-foot birds,
All their softness gone, except in imagination's
Memory. Lilies that fester. I think of Rilke

And wait for pity to come, real compassion,
For this is wrong. These are images of light,
Of higher places, the miraculous. These
Are the singing from other worlds, the poems,
The glory shining round. Demystified, they
Stare unblinking in a clog of dust and cobweb,
Sad forsaken spirits who have filled our books
And paintings, cast gold on our history,

And can never be obsolete, for we all crave
To be spirit, to shuck off the dying animal,
To fly amazed, atheist or believer, in high music,
Transfigured and grateful. We hate
Our gross misshapen entanglements,
Our crude limitations, and look for what
Angels signify — light in darkness, music,
And brightness linking us to something else.

But I wonder if it isn't in some way
Salutary to find places like this
And contemplate how glory turns to dust,
Free flight to helpless immobility.
Perhaps we should know about dead angels,
Dead dreams, dead music, all the airless rooms
Where lambent hopes end up, and beauty, and see
How far we've fallen from the celestial,

How heavy we are, how mired, how *lumpen*.
I don't know. One last look. They smile their dusty
Doll-smiles. The shadows play tricks. A lone fly
Lurches heavily behind a blind. I must leave,
Full of dark obsequies. But then, as
I step outside, bright birds, blue and white and gold,
Unfurl their wings and swoop and soar in a great
Cloud, their songs pealing and belling

In pure enormous harmonies, not strange
To the heart, and I lift my eyes up high to them,
My spirit soft and open to the summer,
And compassion finally breaks for what
Is behind me in that room of death,
Compassion breaks as if I were released,
And it is wide as all the sky and glorious.
I stand astonished, half blinded by the sun.

Saskatchewan

BEDSIDE MANNERS

How little the dying seem to need —
Some food perhaps, an occasional drink,
A smile, a hand to hold, medication,
A change of clothes, an unspoken
Understanding about what's happening.
You think it would be more, much more,
Something more difficult for us
In this massive lurching disruption,
But perhaps it's because as the huge shape
Rears up higher and darker each hour
They somehow think we should see it too
And just try to show us with a hand-squeeze.

We panic to do more for them,
And especially when it's your father,
And his eyes are far away, and your tears
Are all down your face and clothes,
And he doesn't see them now, but smiles
Quietly, perhaps because you're there.
How little he needs. Just love. More love.

NO FLOWERS PLEASE

And now Edith Baker is dead.
Just weeks ago she led me round
Her garden, showed me the long
Symmetry of vegetable
Rows, of fruit, the groomed riot
Of flower beds, all tended quite
As scrupulously as her life.
Day after day she worked out there,
But still had time to visit all
The sick, to listen and reassure.
Even to gossip. She coped well
With crisis, had all the right words.
Edith Baker, age eighty, is dead,
She who showed me round her garden
And then warmly took my arm.
Come dear, come inside for some tea.

Today she left the avenue,
Silently, silkily, in a car
Full of flowers, up the hill.
And the concrete of the road did not
Heave open, trees did not split
And crash or the ground shudder.
An ordinary day, then. But I
Can't accept it. I refuse. I can't
Stop the roaring in my head
And I go out to my own poor garden,
Rip up coloured flowers, scatter
Them high in the air, high to the wind,
Twist and break long thin stems
For Edith Baker, trample the wet
Earth to mark her death. My wife:
Come dear, come inside for some tea.

LATE WINTER, SPRING THREATENING   *for B.*

These evenings light lengthens.
Snow warms and slowly drains
Taking the bitter year with it.
(Ragged, formless all this — holding on
And letting go; warming, freezing;
The moon is neither threat nor comfort.)

And I know you are behind that window
Where the light burns faintly through the night,
Turning your feelings like the seasons,
Feeling the letting-go, the break-up,
The slack of what was firm for you
So short a time ago trickling
Away without pattern. (Oh I know. I know.)

You are still too deep in winter
(I would help you),
But if I tell you that these shapeless days
Will be memory sooner than you think,
That what you feel as guilt and melt
Is really just a huge sadness,
A grief for what had to break and end,
You will not believe me,
Nor let your hands stop twisting,
Your tight throat loosen (the words would stun),
Your eyes open out to distance,
To a future which holds you intact,
Lovely, undamaged, splashed with sun.

MY SON, A BALL, THE YEARS

The phone-call came late
From Edmonton, saying he would
Be taking the milk-run bus
And would be back in Calgary
About six in the morning.
He'd take a taxi home.

Back from playing goal
For the Alberta soccer
Team in the Nationals.
We beat Quebec in the final
And won it all, he says,
Almost as afterthought.

My son, sixteen, cool,
Travelling the night
And summoning taxis.

My son the goalkeeper,
Age four, the day we first
Arrived in Alberta, pleading
For me to unpack a ball
And play a game of catch
With him on the motel grass.

1981

PRAYER FOR MY CHILDREN

There are times in the night when I grieve for them my
children when I almost believe I was wrong to have brought
them here where the rockets rest nervously underground under
the sea where nuclear waste is dumped casually where the
rain turns acid eating the soft globe gently as gently as I
held them once lifting them into soft towels where crazy men
have guns and bombs and faces of hate where the quiet
torturers are always at work asking questions questions
through the screams where the whales and tigers are nearly
gone and I hate it all and know I don't really belong to
their world and don't want to and I know they feel so much
but don't know how to feel in shapes because their world is
all dip and whirl and plunge and noise instead of pattern
which I want and need and they don't think they do because
as children they must reject the shapes of my old longings
my music my books all of us who brought them here and left
them and oh I would raise them high to the huge protecting
moon if I could but the moon is dirty now and space is full
of cameras and weapons and I would I swear it gladly lie on
sacrificial stone and let the knife end me if that would
hold their futures intact shape their raw hopes shelter them
from the eating rain the harpoons of a sour and greedy world
soothe the throb of their longing as they reach out hands
for meaning in all of this for something clean and soft and
gentle that will not hurt for their own quiet shapes to live
in and then in other places minute black sacks of bones lie
eyes still moving waiting the ultimate wait too weak to
reach for anything so can I only pity give money try to be
gentle put words on this paper when it's too little and no
good but far too much to carry and the nights last far too
long and I'm saying save them now and later and I'm saying
keep hope behind their eyes and I'm begging keep hope behind
their eyes behind the softness of their eyes

FROM

Waiting for the Barbarians

1971

POEM FOR JEAN

Your face, those years
ago, shining
like a shell in the sea
of evening. And I,
lost land-creature,
had to lift you.

Today, these many
miles inland,
the world is dry.
There is no shining.
My dear, before
it is too late,
come, we will go
back to the star-
fish and the crab.

WINTER SONG

cold and in the winter weather
comfort is denied
doors are fast but still the weather
rages inside

security becomes survival
timbers creak and stir
between our lives and something evil
a bulging door

tired and in the greyest weather
cold savaging the bone
nightly nightly we grow weaker
and our blood runs thin

lovers kill each others' longing
art and logic cease
between the impulse and the action
a frozen space

enduring in the steady weather
in the snow's long falling
we wait for rescue — a sudden thaw
or voices calling

PAST LOVES

Their bright colours have faded.
One by one they have
Been refined by the years
Until they are no more
Than curiously mingled
Scents, caught only faintly
Yet known for what they are.

Farewell to all of them,
Half-forgotten, but deeply
Part of me, like those flowers
Of a country childhood —
Colesfoot, centaury, loosestrife —
Whose names come back from where
No winters were, nor thorns.

MAGNETS

Safe enough, you think, a field
    Like this, decently wide,
And you like poles at an even distance.
So the slow current is concealed,
    Attraction seems denied,
And space intrudes in case you yield.

Who could foresee that sudden start,
    The force that set these two
Jerking on their helpless course, the shock
Of contact, such connection? Whose art
    Can hope to free them now,
Coupled so close yet poles apart?

IN THE BASEMENT

Check the laundry room
during the day and you'll see them,
washer and dryer, standing quietly
next to each other, a matched pair
minding their own business.
At night it's different.
Under the complacent sleep
of this Calgary suburb
something strange is going on.

It's not surprising.
Think of their frustration
standing day after day
with bare white flanks touching
each throbbing with power
but programmed separately.
No wonder they go mad
when we're not there.

Exactly what they do we don't know —
genial couplings with hoses
switches and cords;
clumsy titanic orgies —
we have never disturbed them.
All we know is that in the mornings
beads of cooling moisture
stand on their gleaming sides,
the basement air is warm,
and on the floor
confused marks of castors
and a sinister trace of suds.

One night perhaps we shall creep
down and surprise them.
But now, our claim to the house less,
we go to bed earlier and earlier.

PHILISTINE AT THE BALLET

I am uneasy here
watching this famous pair
perform their love scene.
The fellow in the tights
worries me most. Suspicious,
my eye goes to his crotch.
Enough there, certainly,
but bound so tightly
you'd think he was trying to hide
some gross impediment.
What denial of assertion!
And she is just as bad
in her silly gauze skirt,
swooning, half-reluctant,
settling like a white
balloon on a draughty floor
to the coy shimmer of fiddles.
Imagine him in bed
with her, stripped of music
and humping her for real . . .
No. And that's what's wrong.

Soon it will be over
and I'll escape. Tall,
awkward, trousers flapping,
clumping on heavy heels,
I'll walk the grey streets
to my untidy flat,
my monstrously pregnant wife,
and the world I live in.

THE ACADEMIC

Charmed by the Disney appearance,
the hint of domestic dogginess
in the brown rheumy eyes, night
after night girls climb his stairs.
Perhaps they go to comfort him,
this stooping scholar with the glasses;
perhaps to sit at wise old feet
and confess some frisky indiscretion.
No matter. Their safety is assured.
No wolf could fake this sort of tameness —
or so they think until he slips
his leash. Then see him speeded up,
jerking in coloured animation,
the cartoon teeth suddenly sharp,
the prey in slightly comic flight,
until, with a flourish, The End.
In the slow black and white of morning,
he lopes to his classroom full of girls.

DRACULA

The story, we feel, starts perfectly —
The brooding Transylvanian landscape,
Travellers, a storm, the inn
With its Brueghel peasants, merrymaking
Forgotten and stiff with superstition,
Grouped around the scrubbed table;
The muttered rumours of strange happenings
In the old castle, low unearthly
Noises in the forest, and, worse,
Of something coming at dead of night
With a bang of shutters to the beds
Of trembling village girls, pinning
Them to stifling sheets and leaving
Two rubies livid on their necks;
Then the dazed village slowly
Gathering strength in the pale morning,
Only to find in the Baroque graveyard
Some hand has thrown the stones aside
And the musty smell of death is there.

But after this what ending is possible?
Surely we are not to believe
That a six-inch crucifix,
Held in pious trembling hands,
Could shrivel like a spent balloon
One whose spreading shadow covered
Half of Europe? Or that a handy
Stake could drive that presence out?
This could not end with evil neatly
Piled in ashes on the floor,
A mild light beaming through the forest,
And peasants dancing in the streets
Miraculously freed from fear.
No. The story went too far.
For even now, at nights, safe
And secret under blankets, I know
The fabulist was wrong when something
Hideous and familiar appears,
Parting the mists and coming towards me.

THE DEAF-MUTE CHILDREN

Surprised by the silence I turn.

All seven are deaf and dumb,
their excited moving hands
making the bus behind me
a cage of wild white birds.
Nervous, I light a cigarette.

Off the bus, through the trees,
I run to meet my son,
words booming in my head,
gestures fluttering in the air.

THE LANCASTER

Silent in the sweet stench
Of seaweed, nose buried
In sand, the Lancaster lay
Derelict, not far from shore.

Each night we heard bombers,
Sometimes a thousand, climbing
Over Yorkshire to the coast.
Berlin, Hamburg, Bremen,
We made our children's guesses
As the engines shook the beds.
We'll hear them coming back.

But this one was unlucky.
Singled from the callous flock,
It came lurching from the night,
Skeleton smashed, wings torn,
Fighting for its landfall.
We didn't hear it hit.

Slowly the persistent sea
Explored the carcase, coldly
Consuming, wearing it away.
And somehow swilling, too,
In my unsuspecting head,
Bringing prophecies of pain,
Like a tide, blank and rising.

AFTER THE ASSASSINATIONS 1968

times like this
I need to be
in the smoke creek
desert nevada
or pelican lake
minnesota

just being there
would be enough
I think
there would be
fabulous animals
to be alone with
and to be strange with
and quietly there
I would melt
in sun
harden in snow
entirely part
of nevada
or minnesota

a man I knew
cured something
in his chest
by going to live
in the mountains
but that's not
what I'm talking
about

THE SPHINX WASP

Attacking yards ahead
of its thin wire of sound,
it has the blank uneccentric
purpose of a missile.
Twisting and diving
it homes like a Phantom
on a flight deck,
trailing its sting
like an arrester-hook.
Finding one dead
you are surprised
it is not painted metal.

The system is neat.
Stung and paralysed,
the spider is dragged
two feet underground
to a prepared chamber
and arranged.
The eggs are laid
and the ravenous larvae
emerge to a whole world
of warm living meat.
Gorging they grow.
When they crawl out,
wasps,
they take off and search
automatically for spiders.

Once, on a patio
in America's heartland,
I watched the process.
For all its running
the spider had no chance.

And today I think of others,
the small frightened ones
half the world away,
who hear American wings
and feel the sickening
blow from the sky.

Blankly, efficiently,
we are storing up corpses
for our children.

LETTERS FROM GLASGOW

The sun is not hot.
It is not a good position I am in.
JOHN BERRYMAN

1. my friend
   sails a yacht
   in geneva new york
   14456
   he goes swimming
   plays softball
   and paints his house
   we were closer once

   for me glasgow
   city of the knife
   addicted to dull
   habits of violence
            50 stabbings
            this easter weekend
   ambulances cruise
   the long streets
   wailing

   sick of poverty
   sick of stone
   sick of shrinking
   and decay
   the people emigrate

   I must escape

   how else
   will I lose
   this slackness
   this slow
   rotting
   of
   nerve

2. forget gentleness
   better be
            hard
            tall
            stone

   treeless
   for miles here
   all inessentials
   are gone
   torn down
   stoned down
   with a thin strength

   and the people
   see how they look
   behind them

   an old god
   lives here
            black
            massive
   blocking the sun

   he holds
   a razor
   and a bottle

3. weather limits us
    and landscape holds us
    here we are caught
    in weather
            thick sullen
    it gathers
    from the atlantic
    and cuts us back

    we drown in greyness
    dominated by
    this grey stone
    these grey people
    and the western
    drench of weather

    we had not wanted this
    but somehow came
    it is hard to remember

    we must break loose

    heart pumping
    the crazy-eyed rabbit
    stares at the headlights
    and thinks and thinks
    of moving

    our landscapes hold us

    frantic exiles
    we come from somewhere
    and we nudge weeping
    into darkness

AT THE RESERVATION

Iowa swells obscenely in the heat.
All around us cornfields, dust and farms
Spill heavily over vague liquid horizons.
Off Highway 6 we take the tourist road
And follow *Sac-Fox Reservation* signs.
The Buick smells of skunk and hot rubber.

Each summer, fatter and more prosperous,
We hunt the plains of this wide land, locked
In our coloured cars, obeying signs and limits,
Pushed forward by some old recurring hunger.
The ghosts are stubborn and our dreams are bad.

I don't recall what we set out to find.
More, I know, than that dirty clapboard town,
Its main drag lined with bars and fading flags
Like the site of some abandoned carnival.
We saw the rugs, the beads, the totem-pole;
The fat-necked tourists and their jewelled wives;
The pimp, fresh out of daddy's farm, who offered
"Red meat" by the railroad tracks for twenty.
In an Indian bar, we watched the greasy-haired
Young braves, in sweatshirts and dirty levis,
Coarsely swilling 3.2 Grain Belt.
Thick and rotten, the day was choking us.

We came away with nothing from that place,
Except that once, across a crowded bar,
I thought I saw an old face through the smoke,
Across whose eyes the memories wandered in herds.

THE VISIT

The scene was too bright from which you came
Stalking stiffly towards us. In a shuddering sun,
Painted drainpipes meshed and bulged like veins
Across the building's coarse Victorian face.
Flowerbeds gaped in the lawn's swollen sides,
Vile as open wounds. Too much brightness.
And you flinched, not with the specific pain
Of snapped bones or torn flesh, but because something
Too bright was inside you, wild and screaming
In your mind's cage like a trapped coloured bird.

You were glad we came. Said it made a difference.
You couldn't know what difference was in us,
Or how, later, making love to your sister,
Trying to tilt our reeling day back true,
A fury overtook me once again,
Beating like wings behind her lovely eyes.

THE GARDEN

They still recall the time
When they made the formal garden
Next to the wall of the jungle,
Separated only by a river.
They remember how the children
Would stand and look across

As if something across
There made them see the garden
Differently. Or perhaps the jungle
Smell on the warm river
Awakened something in the children
Before its usual time.

Whatever it was, that time
The children disappeared from the garden,
Footprints led to the river
And a break in the wall of the jungle.
They thought of going across
But held back in case the children

Should return another way, as children
Do, and find them gone in the jungle.
They waited some time
Then left and went back across
The land, away from the river.
What could they do in the garden

But sit and think of the garden
As it had been with the children?
They found a new house by a new river
And in the garden grew thyme
And forget-me-nots. Across
The country the spreading jungle

Covered the formal garden. Jungle
Creatures prowled where the children
Used to play, crying across
The land as they had in the time
Before they built the garden
And pushed the jungle back over the river.

Now the old ones sit quietly, as across time
Their minds go back over garden and river,
Deep into the jungle, seeking their lost children.

FROM
The Barbarian File
1974

BARBARIAN'S DANCE

under a torn black sky
the world was broken/
everywhere the fields
tilted crazily
and rolled away

desperately
the cracked hills
tried to pull together
their folds and rags

the creatures lay
fallen and curled

the land waited
like the backdrop
for some play which
would strain belief

B got out of bed
stretched shaved
started walking
into the silence

he whistled and smiled
even did a funny
shuffling dance
which stirred the dust
all over that wide plain

and then
the fields straightened
and the sky
grew bright
a tawny sunlight
healed the hills

B smiled shyly

BARBARIAN AGONISTES

something new this time/
fractured
          was he
NO
but bent badly
bruised around the heart
and loins
and his head was wrong
in a new way
he felt apart
and couldn't help it
try the churches
          said some
           trying to help
these things can be shriven
by endless repetition
by sacrifice
and holy water
try the hospital
          said others
they will remake you there
shock it away
with electricity
          (B trembled
          nearly fell)
try love
          they all said
through lips and eyes
gentleness and healing will come
and make you whole
so B tried love
but the bitch
walked out on him

BARBARIAN IN CALGARY

under a pitiless sun
the stores offer their
nourishment

The Popular Beethoven
Mahler Is Heavy
Mozart's Greatest Hits
Switched-On Bach
Sacred Music Hits
by Porter Wagoner
and Dolly Parton

tasteful genuine
Polynesian rumpus rooms

pink flamingos
and Black Sambos
for the lawn

back home
on FM it's
Classical Cavalcade
with Arthur Fiedler
conducting Bacharach
and the Beatles
sponsored by
Mohawk Auto Square
and The Three Green Horns

he sat down
applied for jobs

there were
no replies

THE HORSEMAN

across dusty meadows
and dusty scrub
among a few
shrivelled trees
a tattered knight
on a knackered horse
comes lurching
at a half canter
his exhausted
companion
long left behind
in the dust

his eyes
vague and cloudy
search the horizons

the enemy is elusive
merging with trees
in extreme shapes
lost to sight
in the low liquid sun

he won't give up
urging his old horse
outward onward
round in great circles
and round in small circles

he will tilt at him
tilt and win

day after day
the hooves stutter
around the tiny
painted
landscape

HIS PREDICTION

you said
what will it be like
when we are old
and I told you
how we would sit
in sun and music
under trees
and speak of how things were
when everything was new
and in its place
I said
we would speak
of how long ago
we stood at night
laughing and crying
and tried to catch
the moon in a net

I told you these things
and you smiled and
pretended you didn't know
that all the time
behind my smile
I was thinking of
how it will be
when the moon is gone
when we are alone
when we are nothing
but clothes and bone

HIS DEPARTED FRIEND

he was so dumb he went

to a massage parlour for massage

to Maple Leaf Gardens for hockey

to TV evangelists for religion

to Rod McKuen for poetry

to a Faculty of Education for education

to a psychiatrist for truth

to Europe for bargains

and finally to the United States

for freedom and the good life

so long old buddy I'll miss you

perhaps one day you'll come back

to Canada for flair wit and excitement

REPORT FROM THE IVORY TOWER

the computer told them
of an ongoing shortfall
in student enrolment
of overstaffing and underfunding
of insufficient accountability

he sniggered too soon

he had a small class
they abolished small classes
he was up for tenure
they abolished tenure
he was foreign born
they abolished foreigners
he lectured on Keats
they abolished Keats
he published no papers
they took away his money
he grew a beard
they shaved it off
they sent teaching experts
to observe him
set up committees of scholars
to discuss him

one day
without thinking
he scratched between his legs
and they castrated him
with union observers
following the exact
procedures outlined
in the official
computer-checked
handbook for faculty

THE HUNT

There is no forest or fell to escape to today, no cave in which to curl up, no deserted valley for those who wish neither to reform nor corrupt society but to be left alone.

E. M. FORSTER

The lord will ride

already the grooms
have prepared the great horses
the courtiers donned
the rich hunting clothes
the dogs are leashed
rustics in jerkins
are beating the woods
lining up and moving in

in the heart of the greenwood
B
panting
seeking cover

catches sight
through the oaks
of rich brocades
tapestry colours
flickering around him

he breaks
running
reaches the edge of the wood
the great park
stretching empty ahead
takes a huge breath
runs out in a swerve

behind him
the horns blow
the eager dogs are slipped
flights of arrows
sing in the luminous air

no cover
B zigzags

with a huge belly laugh
the lord reloads
from his jewelled quiver

THE FALL

discovering he could fly
he launched himself from the top
of an apartment block
fell lazily like a leaf
hovered by windows
all over town

and he saw the desperate ones
the marriages going sour
in vicious silence
the artists weeping and selling out
he saw the cruel ones
and a few kind ones with sad eyes
the rebels with their peace
placards and weapons
the very old with their
photographs and medicines
and some children dreaming
themselves out of it all
he saw the dead eyes of scientists
among tumours and cells
and the panting ones
in the flicker of movies

don't worry
he thought to himself
as he hit the sidewalk
his head exploding softly
like a tomato
under a blunt knife
the whole thing's just
a very obvious parable

they came
and shovelled him up

THE QUARTERBACK

that first season
it seemed he could do everything

behind great blocking
he was right on target
with slant-ins and curl-patterns
his occasional bomb arched
inch-perfect into grasping hands

he crossed up defences
with counters and trap-plays
he checked the rush with
perfect screens and draws
his options and bootlegs
were a joy to watch

it went wrong in november
for no apparent reason
he was sacked over and over
his passes wobbled like shot ducks
his screens were read each time
he threw interception after interception

now at 27 he is coaching juniors
going through the motions
his eyes far away
each night trying to persuade
sceptical drunks to go home with him
and look at his scrapbooks

THE PAINTING

always one to
celebrate epiphanies
he painted a woman
of perfect proportions

one hand finely boned
hung slackly
over her groin
the other
a masterpiece of perspective
reached straight out
seeming to beckon

it was fable
it was magic
he knew he had got there
at last
out beyond time

but one day
as he stood in front of it
her delicate hand
reached out and closed
on his wrist and slowly
drew him into the painting
until he was kneeling
at her feet
imploring
upwards reaching
wild with longing

if you find the painting
you will see him there
on the left side
tiny exquisite
so lifelike
you will be
amazed

THE SCULPTURE

took a huge block of marble
and started
wondering why he'd never
done this before
he was pure and relieved
chiselling hammering
out a perfect man
clean bold limbs
gentle shadows
outlining the grace of it
the grace of it

he grinned for months
ignored his bleeding hands
finally hoisted it
with block and tackle
on to its solid base

then suddenly
the arms fell off
the neck snapped
and the head hung askew
a map of cracks
raced creaking over the body
the genitals dropped with a roar
the legs buckled slowly
as if under tremendous weight
until the thing hung
ruined in its chains

and he
sat there in the dust
among the great smooth fragments
until they came for him
and led him dumbly heavily
away

BARBARIAN REMEMBERS AND
LOVES HIS CHILDREN

more and more
these days
old voices and places
turn vacantly
inside his head

he looks forward less

once he had
a kingdom where
the land met the sea
and he ran in it
and shouted at the sea

starfish dripped in his hands

he caught great
dark red crabs
and marvelled
at their slowness

he stared into pools
and was calmly but
sharply reflected

above him contrails
and soft gunfire
in the high clouds
and sometimes bombs fell
near him and his brother
until he thought
his mother would cry
all her life

he founds shells
of white by the sea
and silver shells
from a Messerschmitt
he kept them together

his children in the city
should know all of this
he will tell them
when they wake
afraid of all the noises
he will tell them
how he would wait
in the shining air
for the tide to uncover
its small brittle things

but especially
he will tell them
how he waited
most patiently
for his father
in strange blue clothes
to come home

BARBARIAN IN THE WILDERNESS

B elated with companions on the trail
he was away from the other things

through pines through aimless clouds of butterflies
feet comfortable on grass and soft droppings

claws had ripped the trees there were skulls and feathers
strong B dared nature to wreck him

his friends shouted off a mountain and heard echoes
B shouted just as loud but there was no echo

met a sizeable bear who threatened his friends
saw B and ran in panic

B's friends looked at him
and kept on looking as he stood ankle deep in swamp

covered with flies grinning amiably with big teeth
and occasionally howling like a wolf

THE COUGAR POEM

Knowing cougar were there made him move to the mountains.

All summer he scans the high ledges for what might move.

Grizzly, wolverine, eagle, wolf are of no interest to him.

Not seeing cougar makes them bigger.

Knowing he has been watched by cougar makes him smaller.

The small head and the huge back legs fascinate him.

His dreams are of cougar, of the red inside the mouth and
the unbelievable jumping.

It's always those who don't want to who see cougar.

However far he goes into the back country he will never
find cougar.

He is possessed by cougar.

Back home he pads lightly on springy soles, jumps the stairs
in two bounds.

At his mirror he snarls and hisses, baring long teeth.

Imperceptibly his nails grow longer.

HIS NEW CAR

he's proud of it
this new model
shining in front of his house

sitting in it
electric seats adjust him
backwards and forwards
moulding him to their shape
belts enfold him protectively
the wheel swings into his hands
lights of all colours bathe his eyes
mirrors adjust automatically
warmth rises around him
music swims into his ears
smooth silent power
glides him around town

until one day
riding rich and tall
all systems working perfectly
the car took off on its own
heading through town
far out beyond the lights of people
towards dark roads
unspeakably remote

helpless
strapped in
gas tank showing full
he was carried away
into the darkness
in his cushions and music

so perfect was the soundproofing
that nobody heard his screams

HIS LOVE POEM

an arm
deep
in water
bends
and shines
white
in green
trembles
away its
solidness

so I
with you
in this strange
greenness
bend and
alter

released
from old
forms
changing
trembling
into new

THE QUESTION

long ago
his footprints
were washed
from the sand
at Flamborough

should he
go back
for what he
might see
when the tide
uncovers
the sand

or stay
away
his sleep
each night
breaking
with tides
the salt smell
sweet in
his head
the footprints
young and
arrow-straight
clear in
the sand
at Flamborough?

FLAMBOROUGH HEAD

The heart drains slowly,
Fills again, drains and fills.

Sudden heaves of water
Explore the weakness of soft stone.

I shouldn't come here.
I have been too far away.

It hurts to contain such fullness
And erosion, these long tides

Which rinse the memory.
Yet I have loved this place,

And the draining and filling
Make the chained heart move,

Make time flow strong and dizzy
Through the starved and landlocked mind.

CORNELIAN BAY

The metal yelp of gulls, huge flocks
        of redshanks by the
    lagoon, the big rock, White Nab,
        the suck and slobber
of the mud-patch — nothing has changed.

The eye moves, and the memory.
        By the tide-line worm-
    casts, razorshells, bladderwrack,
        mussels. Some seapinks.
Even the concrete pill-boxes

left from that other time, now used
        as convenient
    toilets on the beach. Once I
        watched them being built,
remember the soldiers swearing.

The black rocks where I cut my knees
        swimming, tidal pools
    clear and green, anemones
        and crabs moving here.
Thirsty, the eye drinks. It all looks

the same. But I turn away. In
        thirty tidal years
    there have been erosions, old
        solids worn away,
and deep down I am undermined.

FILEY BRIG

Back again
under these cliffs.
The sea stretches
tight and grey as canvas
out to a cold curved horizon.
My children wade the pools
searching for crabs.
My mind lets go
and for a moment
I am back thirty years
a child in these same pools
free and running
with the long tides
in the bright weather.

Triumphant, my son
holds up a crab,
his face alight,
wanting my praise.

AT RIEVAULX ABBEY

Rooks and pigeons have it now
And the rain from the high moors
Which followed us down the valley.
It's the size astonishes, and the quiet,

Out in this remoteness. No guidebook
Or photograph prepared us for it,
Suggested this immensity.
Time and weather have been cruel

To the great nave, but still the arches
Soar and amaze. Midwinter.
We are alone on the tended grass
Under the sullen dripping stone,

But suddenly we know we are standing
On generations of the dead, men of prayer
And singing, lying all around
Their massive altered headstone.

Bareheaded we remain among them
In the bird-noise and the drizzle
As time's circle draws us in,
And from the stone there comes

A faint persistent music,
Elusive, half-remembered, celebratory,
As the blowing rain, soft and fine,
Drifts over us like shrouds.

DISUSED AIRFIELD

It would be easier to make sense of this
With a movie camera and a tape-recorder.
The camera would pan slowly, lingering
Over the fields, the burst concrete

Of the disposal bays, purple with willow-herb,
The still solid foundations of Nissen huts,
To the shell of the high control tower,
Windowless, grey, and the ruins around it.

At that point the recorder would start
With a faint hint of excited male voices,
And the film would slowly dissolve
Until the set was new again, in 1942,

Aircrew chatting over pints of dark beer,
Mechanics in fatigues working on the Merlins,
Figures in the tower talking into radios,
Bedford trucks moving around the perimeter.

All would be movement and purpose.
Cut to local village pub. Cut to bombs
On low trolleys pulled by tractors.
Cut to old men and young women

Looking suddenly upward in the streets
As the twilight draws the first bombers,
Climbing, fighting for their element.
Great days, the camera and recorder would say.

Today I stand here alone,
My eyes panning across sluggish cows
Deep in meadowsweet and nettles.
No dissolve. The voices do not come.

And yet, suddenly, how clear my father's
Face, his cap, his blue uniform.
I stay for hours, my only tribute,
Grounded in the airborne song of birds.

THE FIELD

That's where I saw the Lysander crash,
I tell my son,
when I was about your age.
There were two men in it,
both killed.

But it's flat, he says,
just a flat field.
Where's the hole?

I drive on,
hunched tightly around
that scarred place inside me.

TO A GERMAN PILOT

I wonder where you are now, you bastard.
Were you just using up ammunition
When you shot up our street in the middle
Of the night? Or was it impulse, whim,
Orders, some personal revenge?

I see you fat and prosperous with a cigar,
An executive in some booming modern business,
Occasionally telling war stories over schnapps,
Laughing as you show photos of yourself posed
On the cockpit steps of the 110.

But then I may be wrong, and you are lying,
A mess of bone and leather, in a weed-covered
Black fuselage deep under the North Sea,
Or propping up one of those identical
White crosses in a war cemetery.

I know I shouldn't care any more
The way I did then, crouching under
The dining-room table with my mother
And baby brother, blankets over our heads,
Hearing the sky explode over the house.

My hate went up like tracers at you then.
You crippled old Mr. Freeman with a 20
Millimetre shell as he was getting out of bed,
And you hit every house on the street
Except ours at the end of the row.

We were shown some unexploded shells
The next day — silver and red — and told
Not to touch any we found. You bastard.
Were you one of those carefree ones,
The knights of the air, wearing a yellow scarf

And a white smile, singing "Wir fahren gegen England"?
Or a sour loner, prowling the night skies
Like an owl for anything that might move?
Puff your cigar. Roll under the long waves' swell.
Shift slowly under the tended grass.

You hit no military target that night,
But your mission accomplished something
If only that a hundred people would never be
The same. I still dream of you and your black plane.
Because of you I learned to fear and hate.

GRANDMOTHER DYING

We arrived in time, but only just,
Taking the slow wartime train,
The paddle-steamer over the Humber,
The bus to Ferriby, and then
Having to walk long miles to the village
Dragging my four year old brother.

She died sometime the next day.
They laid her out in a bedroom
Of that huge country rectory.
My mother took me to the door
And let me look. My first dead body,
The face yellow against the sheets,

The room more still than any I
Had ever been in. Thick shaded silence.
Afterwards the Lancasters
From Elsham warmed up for the night's
Raid, shaking Lincolnshire's heart,
And I walked off alone in the garden.

Bubbling moans of pigeons drowned
The bombers and I moved around
The outbuildings, the disused grass
Tennis court, sour and deep with nettles,
Feeling no grief, but quiet and solemn
As I knew I was expected to be,

Wanting to help my stricken mother
But having no words.
                    Today I visit
My grandmother's grave, taking my children.
East winds and salt air have rubbed away
The inscription, weathered the soft stone
To a mossy yellow. Impatient, the children

Pull away. For them it might
Have been there two hundred years.

MEMORIAL

Doris Irene Nightingale loved this view
— plaque on a seat overlooking the
South Bay at Scarborough

Perhaps she sat here, deep in age,
Remembering childhood holidays —
Bathing machines and donkeys,
Punch and Judy, carriage-rides,
Palm-court orchestras at the Spa.
Or was it in the worst of times,
Sons or husband in submarines
Or the Russian convoys, she sat,
Letters and photos in her handbag,
Searching the grey horizon,
Keeping a faithful duty-watch?

I think she would be gentle,
Someone who found this curve
Of sea necessary, restorative,
One who concerned herself with time,
For thoughts of time breed here,
Break slowly in the mind's far corners.

I stay, feeling her vague ghost
Loosely hovering, and I contain
And hold this view in a new way.
Not casually now but strongly
My eyes move, and I am open
To sea and sky, to an old lady's death.
Sitting here I am her beneficiary,
But more, somehow a descendant,
Older, grateful, reassured.

I shall look for her grave.

AT THE POOL

Not many even dared to start the climb,
I remember. It meant dodging the old lame
Attendant who never let kids up there.

Forty-two feet I think they said it was,
Into fifteen feet of unheated seawater,
And because of the war there weren't even railings

On the steps or at the top. But those were glory
Days — 1946, and the military
Band playing Nights of Gladness — and I was up

There alone before I knew it, scared
Shitless, my friends signalling it was clear,
And I jumped, I jumped. That smack of soles and palms!

From the cafe and terraces above the pool
A round of cheerful applause from onlookers
And I was a hero. I tell my wife all this.

Today, thirty-eight, sitting on that same
Terrace drinking tea, trying to keep
My children from drawing attention to themselves,

I watch the pool like a hawk, praying
That no sodding little yobbo will try
To show off by going up those steps.

COD FISHING

Cold November nights are best
With the high tide whipped
By a razor wind, the waves
Exploding like shells on the rocks.

Like tonight.
The fingers can hardly grip
To put the lugworm on
To control the huge cast

Over the seaweed and rocks
Eighty yards with luck
Right into the big combers.
You can't see where it goes.

And then it's waiting,
The bell on the rod whirring
In the gale, hands useless
In pockets, face frozen,

The white sea in the blackness
And some white stars
Between low cruising clouds
And the tide getting round you

And the rod-tip jerking
But only with the wind
With vibration from the breakers
Though the numb heart jumps.

Likely as not this is all
You'll ever get.
Likely as not this is all
You could ever stand.

THE SISTERS

She brings you in for tea,
Though she hardly knows you,
Offers thin cucumber sandwiches
With no crusts, cut in quarters,

And sitting by her electric fire
Introduces you, finally,
To her loony older sister.
The room smells of lavender

With a trace of face-powder.
There's a gormless budgie.
The sister says nothing, but works
Her fingers incessantly, smiling

And nodding. She talks about
The weather, the neighbours, prices,
You answer a little loudly
And very clearly, but mainly you listen

As she tells of of the days between
The wars when she was a singer.
Incredibly she breaks into cracked song —
Something from an operetta.

The half-wit cackles. The clock ticks.
Damn them, these old women.
After being with them
Your own house mocks you,

Empty of voices, empty of music.

THE SHOP

Restrained to the point of gloominess, lurking
Between Smith's and a coffee-shop, it declares itself
With dated gold lettering in black glass:
Greensmith and Thackwray: Indian and Colonial
Outfitters since 1845.
Through the door you can catch glimpses of dark oak
Counters and sober elderly attendants.

Austere and discreet, it wears its breeding well.
It would take courage to walk in there, as once
They must have, the intrepid ones, come
To fit out for the hostile foreign sun.
What blood it must have stirred in frozen hearts!
What promises of remote and glorious arrivals!
Today the windows are full of Shetland sweaters,

Thorn-proof tweeds, stout purple brogues, the better
Regimental ties, the odd deerstalker.
The rich still come here, pale progeny
Of formidable grandparents, in their sheepskins
And Jaguars, but they are fewer now,
Their white moustaches increasingly astounding
Among the macs and plastic shopping-bags.

Surely the place can't last, can't survive
The levelling down, the country's long slackening.
But before it's taken over by some chain-store,
Its guts ripped out to make self-service counters,
It stands as monument, changing a street,
Attracting stares, challenging assumptions,
Insisting on history's sharp realities.

I've never been inside. It's not my style.
But I like to think that when they knock it down
They will find, locked and dark in the back,
A forgotten storeroom, a musty secret shrine,
Lined with bush-jackets, jodhpurs, polo-gear,
Knee-length linen shorts, and in one corner,
Proud, sad, talismanic, a yellowing pith-helmet.

FAMILY REUNION

I put Brylcreem on my hair that day
For the first time. I must have been 13
And trying to rise to the occasion.

The hotel at Southport was full of vague
Cousins and old ladies smelling of wintergreen
And mothballs, adjusting their hats,
Leering through false teeth and crooked lipstick.
I blushed and kept escaping, smelling
My hair, body and tongue awkward.
I remember watching my father
Moving easily around, telling them
All what they wanted to hear.

A lunch of grey beef. Some relative
From Lancaster lit a cheap cigar;
A tug-boat owner from Newcastle
Lectured me on moral values, whisky
Urgent on his breath; the women fluttered
Like tipsy jackdaws. I tried to smile —
A fixed adolescent rictus
Under the caked and reeking hair.

Afterwards, in the car, my father lit
A Craven A and amazed me by saying
With a calm and utter vehemence
"Thank God that's over. Never again."
And I was released, free to go back to my life,
To get my suit off and wash my hair.

There's never been another reunion,
Though for weeks the letters came saying
How marvellous, how interesting, we must . . .
They're all dead now, my mother tells me,
Or nearly dead.

     Since that day
I have never put anything on my hair.
Later that week I had my first cigarette.

IN HIGHWEEK CHURCHYARD

On a mild day, under sun, the moor
Is static and the sea like a postcard,
Too posed, too perfect.

Days like this are better, the November
Sea lost in the weather, clouds falling
Low and thick off Hay Tor,

The trees cold against the grey stone.
The grass thrashes. If it were longer the graves
Would be drowned, lost;

But it is right in this high place,
Right that it should be left alone
To grow and move.

With my mother I stand, cold, northern,
A foreigner in all this Devon wind,
Yet comfortable, at home

Here where a long convergence has ended.
Taking her hand I am proud and tall,
Defined sharply.

High up here, high and strong, I am first-born,
And what if I am crying as I feel
The day, the wind, the clouds,

Our unspoken hopes, our immense memories
Narrowed and contained by the words at our feet:
Stephen Wiseman 1907-1971

REMEMBERING DORSET

Too far. We've come too far.
The heart needs its woodlands
Or it falters, closes, hardens.
We crawl under a white sky
Remembering leaf-mould, woodsmoke,

Birdsong in the mild air.
The heart has need of them
So it can take root, can
Spread, soar and arch, can wind
All round this blighted star.

FIFTY YEARS ON

The camera caught it. 1909 and you
With Florence on the beach at Aldeburgh,
Sitting in your suit and hat, looking
Not out to sea, but slightly downwards,
Your eyes unfocused, as if it were all over
And nothing mattered. Or were you travelling time?

It was time, wasn't it, time that hollowed you?
Twist as you did it held and taunted you,
Sharp memories tearing at the worn heart.

A fierce winter. As I write, Dorset is under snow,
Black spectral trees rearing like gibbets
Over blank and neutral widenesses.
Drifting snow. Drifts of time. An altered place
With Egdon shrunk, the furze and woodsmoke gone.
Grandchildren of rustics sit in council-houses
And watch the world explode to fragments
On rented colour television sets.
The churches are empty, rotting in the weather.

Fifty years on and time has not been kind.
You told us, Hardy; you knew and told us
Something had turned the wrong way.
Nations are broken. Our poetry doesn't rhyme.
Stone crumbles, wood decays, people are diminished.
And instead of finding grey and green felicities,
We live with rancour, betrayal and loss,
With all the sour appalling coincidences.

We falter forward. Time cackles and grins.

THE SHRINE

Early in the morning they start to gather,
Drawn from the world of suffering to this place.
Languages collide and bruise each other
As buses and planes from all Europe and beyond
Arrive and unload their pathetic human freight.
Ash-white children with stick limbs, held by hefty

Sweating fathers, their eyes peering stupidly
From blankets, mingle with the not so bad —
The limpers with sticks and crutches; the half-paralysed;
Those with withered arms or knotted hands;
The deaf, the blind, the dumb, the idiots.
But worst are those in stretchers and wheelchairs,

Lined up as if to start a sprint at a school
Sports-day, wincing at the shock of the sun, some
Carrying dying flowers, some working rosaries
With white urgent fingers. What are they doing?
What does it mean, this gathering here each day
Where once somebody said she saw something?

That folk still long to go on pilgrimages?
It's more than that, their faces tell you. They come
All believing that a generous God will choose
Them personally for his special favour,
Will single them out for that one great miracle
They have pinned all their hopes and money to.

Among them move the pedlars, selling phials
Of holy water, postcards, plastic statues.
Some nuns pass, rustling. The best clothes wilt.
But then they push into the shrine itself,
Jostling, shoving, coming close at last
To the end of their journey. They move like a swelling tide.

The air is full of incense and garlic. Confused,
They try to keep in line, but all order
Is lost as blind compulsion takes them.
Stewards try to hold them back, waving
And shouting, as if such words and gestures now
Could stop their endlessly coming and endlessly going.

THE MATCHSTICK MEN

Here are the matchstick men in the little square,
Some with canes or matchstick dogs, walking
Or standing in groups. Tiny matchstick children
With iron hoops (for this is not today)
Flit about among the thin dark legs.

They are uncountable, these stick people,
And featureless, unless you look closely.
Behind them rears their world — gigantic
Square brick factories where they spend their days,
Mean houses in their shadows. Haze. Cobbles.

They are caught in hardness and straight lines,
In a grey pen under smoking northern skies.
So many of them. So poor they seem, yet
How important on this day of freedom,
How their dignity defies the squalid backdrop

As if they were the countless dead come back
To taste the air again, to find old friends, to talk.
We don't ask what they are doing or why they
Are there. It is enough to recognise them.
But they ignore us, being so busy, and go about

Their business with a sober dignity
We can't help but be impressed by, and, looking,
We are being drawn into their matchstick world,
Perhaps for ever, and it doesn't matter because
They are so earnest, so utterly believable,

So much like us, our own gathered kind,
That it is right that we should join them,
Huddling in groups to reassure ourselves,
Talking, gesturing urgently, shuffling,
Moving with them away from the dark narrow

Streets of our past, solid, massed and drab
On our matchstick legs, in an endless procession
Out of the frame, into the uncertain present,
Where, in case we get too serious, children's
Cries, ringing hoops and barks tickle our ears.

L. S. Lowry d. 1976

AUTUMN LOVE SONG

Since you came to me
And the weather flared and danced,
We have lived as never before,
Have watched each year the leaves
Grow strong and fall, tired
And brittle, to a wonder
Of gold around our feet.

Can such memories fade?
Never. Never. No, not
Even when we lie
Together, past all season,
Touching ankle and shoulder,
Nudging deep underneath
Our shifting bedspread of leaves.

FROM
An Ocean of Whispers
1982

TWO RIVERS

Salisbury, England

Needing reflection, I am drawn to water.
This river is old, grey, sliding silent,
Nudging soft earth banks
Reeking with weed and flower. A slow
Reluctant flatland river, boring perhaps
Under low rain clouds, undramatic,
But let its rhythms grip you and it
Will be a place to return to.
Let your mind sink down to meet its depths
And you will know yourself in the swirl
And shudder of your reflection.
Frantic swallows make sound.
The river trembles, makes no sound.
I have come back.

But even here I can't escape.
The Bow, its primitive ravings and roar,
Deafens the pastures. The pulse responds.
Down from its green glacier and polished lake
It rips viciously into the mountains,
Flashes cruel in a huge crude sun,
Takes the breath, leaves the self behind.
Grizzly and cougar prowl its banks.
There is spilled blood under the peaks,
Elemental things which overwhelm.
No reflection in the shock of water,
No meadows, just rock and pine
And a surge and fury which flatten the senses.

Exiles and homecomings.
Reflections.

By the Avon I stand, a grey-green ghost
Haunting quiet willows, seeking.
Across the fields a medieval spire.
A signpost beckoning.
A path to somewhere I'm not going to.

I wait and hope for balance
While the Bow and all Canada
Tears and slices at the banks of my mind.

AT FORT QU'APPELLE   *for Joan*

Fort Qu'Appelle, Saskatchewan.
Foreign to me.
Place of Indians and Oblate Priests.
Standing in the Church of St. John,
Built in 1885, built
The year men marched north
From here to fight a war.
A dry May. Drought. Dust.
I find a plaque in the church wall.

In loving memory
Pilot Officer Peter Donald Graham Stuart
RCAF attached 19 Squadron RAF
Born Fort Qu'Appelle, January 29, 1918
Missing over the North Sea, August 29, 1941

Here, of all places, the centre
Of another history, another war,
My life is thrown straight at me.
August 1941 he died in the North Sea.
August 1941 I lived by the North Sea,
Played and swam in its grey cold,
Watched the warplanes, counted them
Going out and coming back, identified them.
I remember my father
When he was a Pilot Officer.

Then later in the hilltop cemetery,
Sweet with lilacs and May blossoms,
By the infant graves, a grave from Batoche,
I find a cross and stop again.

Reg Bates from Macclesfield, England.
Died of typhoid 1910.

And I lived near Macclesfield, too,
Knew it well. I hear his English accent,
Flat, northern, echoing mine.

Wars, disease. Memorials, graveyards.

High on this dusty hill,
From deep in a stone wall,
Half the world from Cheshire and the North Sea,
I am reached for by the past.
I am welcomed by the dead.

THE MAN IN OAK BAY

He was in corvettes during the war
In the North Atlantic, on convoy duty
From Halifax. Survived two sinkings
And days in a lifeboat. Still has
His cap and his navy duffle-coat,
Though today he wears a dark blazer
And a crested tie. His accent
Is vaguely British, his bearing proud.
Now that his wife is dead, children gone,
He spends most of his time gardening,
Reading, looking out to sea.

Typical, you think. A relic, out
Of place in the new American Canada
With his umbrella and folded newspaper.
But watch him. Listen to him.
He knows better than us what lurks
Beneath our lives; still feels the plunging
Miles beneath his polished shoes.
He can tell us, if we don't ignore him,
How suddenly the klaxons can scream,
How quickly in the darkness next to us
Black and dripping shapes can break the surface.

IOWA REMEMBERED

I have sat under the trees
Of Iowa on summer evenings
Patient in the hot shadow
Watching early fireflies

And have seen the liquid sun
Spill across long fields.
Nowhere else, nowhere,
With such fertility,

Such endless heaviness.
Red barns, black soil, crickets,
The dry idle clacking
Of cornfields, the faint smell

Of skunk and hot oil from
A distant highway, the sad
Snoring of a tractor
Are part of it, I remember.

Nowhere else such sweetness
In the ground, such a sense
Of fullness, such a gathering
Of riches before night.

Gone from there, I hold
Heartland inside me still.
I have sat under the trees
Of Iowa and been content.

SAMPLER

Young girl, old ancestor,
You would never have thought
That this exercise you had to do
Would have survived and floated
Down the long generations,
Been so prized, so jealously guarded.

To you it was hours of squinting,
Of pricked and aching fingers,
Scoldings, cold rooms, oil-lamps.
It must have taken weeks
Of your life, but it was part,
They would have firmly told you,
Of every girl's accomplishments,
If she wanted to marry well, get on,
To be an expert at embroidery.
And so you went through your paces —
The alphabet, upper and lower case,
The numbers up to fourteen,
A religious motto, rhymed and pious,
And an intricate flowered border
In red and green, spaced perfectly,
Surrounding, as your final touch,
A cheerful over-large bird
On a tiny symmetrical tree.

Ann Platts finished this work when seven
years and half old at Sproxton School
taught by Constance Wollarton
April the 28 1810

You did it and it's on my wall,
Thin as rice-paper, some holes in it,
The gilt frame chipped and faded.
It couldn't stand repair.
So young you were, but you've
Preserved yourself, created
A small, humble immortality.

Young girl,
Your needle pearls blood on my heart.
Old ancestor,
I thank you for reaching to me,
For binding with your bright threads
A family across the centuries.

I am your descendant, Ann,
Far away,
Useless with my hands.

THE ASH TRAY

I have it now,
Keep it by the stereo,
Its tarnished brass plate turned
Towards the room, just legible:

From the teak of H.M.S. Iron Duke
Admiral Jellicoe's Flag Ship
Jutland 1916

It was my father's,
And I remember it
In the hearth by the coal fire,
Its wood sometimes dark,
Sometimes golden in the flames.

I don't use it as an ash tray —
I have so little of my father
That it would seem wrong
To add to the marks he left
So casually on it — but
I see him, year after year,
Bending from a fireside chair,
Finding it without looking,
Banging out his pipe,
And because of that
The cork centre is scorched,
Cracked, worn down, gouged,
And black marks stain the teak.

I have it now,
Its active life over,
As if the flagship from dreadnought
Broadsides had turned, pulled
Out of line, and battered, holed
And burned, carrying its dead,
Limped back through long slow seas
To safe anchorage and its home.

MY UNCLE

He sits at his desk in the wood and leather study, smoking his pipe,
calm, preparing a sermon, writing letters. Every morning I find

him here. Through eighteenth-century windows lawns and trees
stretch and spread. The study is cool. There's a small coal fire.

He was digging vegetables at dawn in gardening clothes, but now
he's in a dark suit and collar. When he's finished he will visit

in the parish. My aunt is in the huge stone kitchen with the cats.
The rest of the house is mine, its empty hallways, empty rooms,

to play in, to be frightened of, to be secret in. Waste paper.
Smells of must, disuse. Old flowered tatters of wallpaper.

It is wartime. I killed two rabbits with a stick as the reaper
cut the wheatfield down to a small square and they finally ran.

Meat for supper. At night the furnaces of Scunthorpe light up
the blackness. So did Hull when it was bombed. I was born there.

I often go down to the apple cellar, to the cold sweetness,
the drawers of fruit, to the smell that tells me life will be golden.

Or to the village shop and its sudden smells of tobacco, spices,
coffee, paraffin, its glass jars, its red and silver bacon slicer.

Sirens. Gas masks. Bombers based nearby. A searchlight battery.
And I in my uncle's study watching him work, waiting for my life.

Such things have shaped me, catch me unaware, tease my dreaming.
Now it's peacetime and I'm at war with myself, and I'm undone

when I catch the smell of apples, of empty rooms, of forked soil.
O uncle, my life, your old age. Sit at peace in your pipesmoke.

MY MOTHER TONIGHT

In streets without children live the old,
And you among them. No human noise
Except for the gentle heeltaps of one or two
Out for their slow daily stroll or heading
For the grocery shop on the corner,
Admiring the flowers as they pass.

You are alone tonight
And every night, and all around you
Are others who are alone. Widows
Populate this place, quiet widows,
Though there are still a few men
Being nursed or pottering in the gardens.

It is a place of birds, their song
Riding over the old people,
Whose lives are lived out and concluded
To their bright clear music,
Soaring high, high and arching.
You watch them, feed them breadcrumbs,

Leave out and refill bowls of water,
For that is a way of feeling useful,
Like cutting back the grass, the flowers,
In this green and fertile landscape
Where growth seems to mock old lives.
You have nothing else to plant, to mould

To your ways. Nothing for all the long years.
You walk feather-light on life's surface,
Uninvolved now with anything of weight
Except grown children and memories.
Each day you wait for the mail, the phone —
Your lifelines in a barely moving sea.

In your mind it must be different.
There I know you still move far, still look
After people, have him there beside you.
There your footsteps are loud and strong,
Ringing the ground, turning heads.
But that is in your mind as you bend

To deadhead a flower, make some tea,
Talk kindly to a neighbour
About an illness or some new trouble.
The birds sing round you. I picture you tonight.
You are lonely in a street without children,
Old and alone, and your face is dear.

CALGARY 2 A.M.

In spite of the fact that it's twenty below
and winter has gone on for six months

in spite of being starved   starved almost to death
for greenness and warmth   flowers and birds

in spite of the deadness of endless classrooms
shopping centres   television programmes

in spite of the pain in the gut   the migraines
the wakings   the palpitations

in spite of the sad knowledge of laziness
of failure to meet obligations

in spite of all these things   and more
I have to report that the moon tonight

is filling the house with a wild blueness
my children grow   excel   are healthy

my wife is gentle   there are friends
and once in a while a poem will come

In spite of the fact that it's twenty below
tonight I smile   Summer bursts inside me

THE THREE OF THEM

I see a woman walking down the street.
She is going to the harbour.
With her are two children, both boys.
They are taller than she is. They don't speak.

She goes to the boats, talks to the fishermen.
She is carrying a small package.
Her face is troubled and a little pale.
Her eyes are quiet with lines around them

From some strain, for she is not old. They climb
Down into a small boat, her children
Helping her, and the fisherman starts
The engine and heads out to the open water.

The three of them stand quietly, holding
The boat's rail, looking back at the land.
The sea is calm. Out in the bay she speaks
To the fisherman and he stops the boat

And stands still, watching her, as she bows
Her head for a moment, then takes the package
And gently scatters its contents
Over the side. The two boys hold her

For she is weeping, silently, with open eyes.
And they watch as the ashes drift on the green,
Drift on the deep deep green, filter down,
Down into the green, where all is moving,

Down to the deepest places, deeper than her eyes.
The motor starts. The boat returns
To the smell of tar, of nets, of fish,
And the man helps them off and shakes her hand,

Bowing his head in a sudden rough way.
And she walks away from the sea,
Not looking back, not speaking, holding
Her sons' arms. Walks off out of sight.

The sea is serious. The great sea moves
Under banks of low grey cloud. Under
The cries of cruising gulls it moves.
I am fragments. That woman is my wife.

AFTER WATCHING THE T.V. EPILOGUE

Around three in the morning,
Before the station signs off,
He is given his five minutes.

Who watches him, you wonder —
Nervous teenagers after making out?
Old insomniacs with vague chronic pains
Waiting patiently for the dawn?
His family and friends?
It can't be many.

And it's bad. It's badly written,
Badly read, the face earnest
But just a bit too sincere,
The eyes constantly shifting
From cue-card to floor-manager,
Looking for some sign.

The living Christ is with you all,
He says.
With Him the night is never dark,
He says.
In Him you can never be alone,
He says.
And his lonely hunted eyes plead
Out at us as if he would like
To apologize for all this,
For keeping us awake,
For having us see him this way.
We are all brothers and sisters,
He says,
And his wide smile becomes fixed
As the pious music swells
And his face is kept on too long
Before they fade him out.

He'll be back again tomorrow,
Deep in the night's furthest corners,
Sincere, uncomfortable, exposed,
Begging us to be his friends,
Saying that nobody is alone,
That there is no darkness,
There is no darkness.

DELAYING TACTICS

I think about where I'd really like to be.
Europe, perhaps — Holland sweet with flowers
And witty with lace; sipping brandy
At Zermatt in a high Alpine cafe;
Sailing past the Drachenfels.
Or somewhere more exotic, more remote,
Like Patagonia, finding small scaly creatures
In the rocks; Galapagos with turtles and birds;
Diving some deep green lagoon for shells;
Drinking coconut milk and eating
Suckling pig tenderly wrapped in leaves.
Or would it be the East, the heat,
Exploring fetid rivers in a leaky junk;
Discovering old temples buried deep
In jungle, shining with snakes and jewels.
Antarctica, the white, the endless white . . .

It's no good.
She knows what I'm doing.
I give in and let it happen,
Opening my astonished eyes to the same
Old shell-shocked bed, the familiar walls,
The slow suburban cars outside.

THE FIGHTER PLOTTERS

for Dennis

R.A.F. Chenies, 1955-1956

When we were posted there they laughed at us.
It was the St. Trinian's of radar stations,
They said, rebellious, a place of losers

And lunatics. They were right. The station
Was supposed to guide fighters to their targets
And see them safely back to base control.

Huge incongruous steel aerials
Turned and nodded in their farmer's field,
We put coloured arrows and counters on tables,

Logged conversations between controllers
And pilots, gave fixes to lost Meteors.
At least that's what they thought we were doing.

Instead, for two suspended years, we made
The craziest Carry On movie of all.
A cast of hundreds with no plot or director.

What actors! Tom Symes, billet farting
Champion, who did the Times crossword
In ten minutes flat. Evil-eyed, sallow,

He calmly told of having screwed his newest
Girl on the Mayor's throne in a midnight
Council Chamber somewhere in South London.

Taffy Wills who stole the C.O.'s Vanguard
And, pissed as arseholes, rolled it in a ditch.
He screamed with laughter when they arrested him.

146

Big Con — oh God! — envied and admired:
"Flash it, Con! Cor, it's like a baby's arm!
Fuckin' 'ell, it's like a young sapling."

(Con's couplings with Dirty Dot in Bovingdon
Were rehearsed in graphic detail every night.
God only knows how she could take him on.)

Dennis, in his own world, whistling Mozart
Above the noise from games of nine-card brag.
Gerry, now in Ethiopia.

And more. And more. And the whole crazy lot
On buses, roaring out *The Good Ship Venus*
And *She Stood on the Bridge at Midnight* to startled

Hertfordshire at 3 a.m. after night watch.
Even the C.O.'s flies hung wide open
Whenever he bothered to walk about the place.

I think of them and wonder. Where have they flown,
Those who measured out the flights of others
With lines and arrows on screens and huge tables?

What gigantic loops through sunlit skies
Have they made, what stalls and unexpected turns,
What landings in soft domestic fields,

In prisons or institutions? Who has been watching
And controlling them through all the years,
Plotting their direction, strength and speed?

From what deep blacknesses of lost nights
Have they called out in confusion for a fix?
Did anybody sane give them an answer?

THE STAMP COLLECTION

You never thought to see me again,
Nor I you, but time washed me up at your door
And suddenly I knew I had wanted to find you.
Needed to after thirty years.

God, I was scared of you then,
More scared of you than of the Germans.
You were bigger than my mother, much bigger,
And fiercely stopped us, your son and me,
From making any noise when we played
Around that big house on the hill
Because your husband, strange, unfit for war,
Was upstairs every day "doing his stamps,"
Up in the foreign lands of his obsession,
A place I had nightmares about.
One sound and he was downstairs in a fury.

But look at us now. I'm six foot two
And you are small and shrunken,
Those hard features run loose on your face.
Seventy, unwell, you live alone, but down the hill
From that big house you had to sell.
Your clothes are dowdy, the furniture old.
Husband long dead, your son, my friend,
A hundred miles away, your days go round
Like tethered donkeys plodding in a circle.
You make me coffee with clumsy arthritic hands
And talk of how happy those long war years were.
I sit remembering; suddenly ask you about the stamps.
Then you draw back shoulder and head the way I remember,
Your voice turns loud and harsh, you point upward
And say you have the collection still, that he
Worked on it until the day he died.
You keep it in the attic, your big investment
For the future, though you can't get up there now.

And I'm undone, scared of you again,
Scared of upstairs, of the loyalty that makes you
Stand guard still, can turn you into what you were.
You grow before me. I shrink and whisper,
Glancing up toward the attic, remembering dreams.
Frightened as a child, I leave the house on tiptoe,
Make no noise with the garden gate.

THREE VARIATIONS FOR EMMA

1. You in all that crowd.

The west country evening
Warm and still outside the hall
And you there, lips half-parted,
Drinking the music.

You and music. And I watching.

I never knew girls like you
With hair like yours,
With names like yours.
I knew a different kind.

You sit in a pool of brightness.

You dazzle, disturb me.
For years I longed for you
As if longing would never stop.
Not moving, I reach and hold you.

The calm swell of music.

Now I contain you,
My eyes carnivorously gentle.
Yes. I have you now.
                    I curse
The years which dried me.

You. You in all that crowd.

2. I know you, Emma Scattergood,
     You're Lucky Jim's Christine;
   The kind I'd only heard about
     Had never even seen.

   You're lovely, Emma Scattergood,
     Your eyes are long and bright
   As you listen to the orchestra
     Transform the summer night.

   You don't know, Emma Scattergood,
     That I even know your name,
   That I watch you push your hair back
     And sit silent, full of rhyme.

   You're mine now, Emma Scattergood,
     Absorbed and part of me.
   My tired mind has clutched and held,
     Will never set you free.

   I love you, Emma Scattergood,
     This night is changed for me.
   But Emma, dear, you're just fifteen
     And I am forty-three.

3. Your name is lovely, Emma Scattergood,
   And your face lovelier. I watched you there
   In half-profile for hours.
                           You liked the concert,
   I liked your hair, not quite blonde, not brown,
   Your young breasts, your hands quiet in your lap.
   You and music. You, Emma Scattergood.

   Another Muse, another one to think
   About, to feed on in the darkest hours.
   You and poems and music. The Emma Muse.
   Hungry, I gather you as the years weigh down.

   I sat behind you, Emma Scattergood.
   In the bright space between us time sat sneering.
   Not yet, but soon, you'll recognize that smile.

HOTEL DINING ROOM, LONDON

I count sixteen others scattered
In this room for dinner. All men.
All alone. Not a woman or child.
Separate tables and total silence
Except for the quick soft rattling
Of one man's evening paper, the sudden
Self-conscious clack of utensils.
The occasional waiter ghosts past me.

There's a Frenchman, an American,
A balding man from Lancashire.
This I know from hearing them order.
The others are too far away,
Floating in still pools of isolation.
One has an impressive Guards tie,
Or something like it, and the best
Suit in the room. Another one
Looks as if he's here to haunt
The British Museum, his corduroy
Jacket human and reassuring.
But even he won't meet my eye.

In the high room we eat steadily.
The silence is strange — muffled
And enclosing, as if the place had been
Built to keep the world right out.
We sit like specimens under glass,
And I wonder just who they all are,
If they are moving from or towards
Something, if their reasons for being
Here are crucial or casual, if they
Have families round other tables.
It would be good to talk.

No matter. I'll forget their faces.
But I'll remember this quiet evening,
Some people brought for an hour into
My life for me to wonder about
Before memory releases them.

Meanwhile we eat. We are alone
At this odd junction of time and place,
Strangers at the hub of Empire.

I catch an eye and quickly look away.

EAST END HOTEL, CALGARY

The days are long.
Some go to the diner for a two-hour breakfast,
Or walk to the laundromat, the store, the bar.
Some stay in their rooms, curled in bed
Or sitting in old stained chairs.
They peer out at the city behind speckled
Brown blinds, count their money, try to mend
Clothes, eat cold food, or visit down the hall
To find an audience for their embroidered
Reminiscences, their worn-out stories of past
Achievements, of youthful bravado, the only way
They have now to impress, assert themselves.
Some pull things out of scarred dressers,
Pore over photographs, newspaper clippings,
Their dreams, their pasts in cardboard boxes.
Some have locked tin trunks opened only when
The calendar is right or the drink is on them.
Some clean their rooms as if for important visitors.

At night you hear them everywhere —
Persistent coughing, rattling snores,
Slow shuffling steps, toilets flushing,
A kettle boiling, the irregular thud thud thud
Of a tapping foot, a faint mouth-organ
Playing the same tune, the same tune.
The air itself feels full of loss,
Of loneliness turning round and round itself,
Being discovered, explored, exhausted.
This is the place where lives leak away.

But do they try to convince themselves
That it's not all over, sit in dressing-gowns
And worn slippers planning some sort of future?
And when one dies, or the men come for another,
Do they welcome it as a break in routine,
A change in the thin faded pattern of days?

When it does happen,
People strip the bedclothes,
Pile belongings into garbage bags,
Give the room a quick clean
And a disinfectant spray.

It takes them fifteen minutes.

ELVIS DEAD

In a rented Dodge, driving
Down Gorge Road in Victoria,
I heard it on the radio.
Elvis is dead.
        I thought I had
Forgotten you but I was shaken.

You reached me.
Back more than twenty years
You reached me, when the sudden
Cruel drive of voice and guitar
Scattered the sweetness of violins,
Stirred rebellion in the blood.
We thought it would all
Last for ever, I suppose —
Doris Day in long party dresses,
Guy Mitchell, Dinah Shore
Telling us over and over
That we were fine,
That things were easy.

You ripped it apart. Ripped it
In a way we couldn't believe.
Exploded it.
What you stood for
Threatened more than comfort.
I imitated your records
With three chords
On an old Spanish guitar.

Now I find and play them,
Worn almost to bits,
And feel again the power
Of being twenty, feel the room
Expanding, marvel at it.
I still know the words.

Scruffy kid.
Fat rich boy.
You changed our rhythms,
Shook the walls of the world.

ELEGY FOR BING AND THE DUKE

Yes, I'll write for you,
Though not many will, I think,
Not poets at least.
I wouldn't have liked you
But I write because you've been part
Of my life for as long as I can remember.
And now you're dead, you who
Shaped an English kid's picture
Of an America which was never there
But which might have been
And now without you couldn't be.

What do I recall?
The thin-faced hero of Stagecoach,
Red River, She Wore a Yellow Ribbon;
Flying Tiger, Marine, FBI agent,
Sub-commander, Fighting Seabee;
You and Victor McGlaglen punching
Each other out all over Ireland.
You were everything America wanted
And to the end you kept providing —
The cowboy with the paunch and croaky voice,
The old gunfighter still destroying evil.
They struck a special medal
For you when you were dying.
I winced, but secretly I was glad.

And Bing, ears sticking out,
The child-like mournful face
Breaking on cue into a knowing grin.
Lifeline to an age of innocence.
Everyone's favourite priest, holy
Yet mischievous. I remember
A great duet with Sinatra,
The timing of your jokes with Hope.
Ease. Panache. Golf was the right game.

Rich men. Arrogant. I don't care.
You helped shape me and I'll remember.
And now goodbye to you both,
Dying as the script intended —
Cancer and heart-attack —
All-American to the end.

THE SOLITARY

From his park bench
He watches them come nearer,
Stopping every few yards to kiss,
And whispering, always whispering.

No more than seventeen,
He thinks, drinking in the girl's
Brown legs, her bare neck.
They pass as if he weren't there.

Later he eats supper,
Looks at his photograph albums.
Legs. Smiles. Where are they now?

All that night,
Soft and sleek
In the dark bedroom,
The weasel envy, the weasel age,
Leaping and twisting.

THE EXPATRIATE

What are you doing here, I want to shout,
You, so English, so polite, among rough farmers
Come off the land to make good; you, of all people,
In Calgary, Alberta, among the oil-men,
The blue-jeaned tearaways in cowboy boots.

Your eye sees the place for what it is.
At times, unguarded, your tongue rakes flesh off it.
Yet you stay, and we sit in your dining room lined
With silver cups and prizes won for golf,
A calendar of Dorset on the wall.

You never speak about the war unless
I push you when you've had a gin or two,
And then you look away, your altered eyes
Reflecting blood-soaked dunes and rolls of wire.
The medals stay locked in a bedroom drawer.

Fish out of water? I've heard them say it.
If they knew! If they knew those Yorkshire backstreets
Where you grew up. If they knew what stalks your dreams.
If they knew how your gentleness and courtesy
Come not from books but machine-guns and grenades.

WOMEN WAITING

You see them at their windows,
Women waiting. Often
They are old, women alone,
And you realise that waiting
Is the worst thing there can be.
Waiting means putting all the long
Past in storage, investing
What little is left in absence.
Whatever they wait for, however
Much they once were loved,
They are alone, utterly.

Do women wait more gently
Than men, more quietly
Inside themselves? Surely not,
Although it seems that way,
Perhaps because there are so many
Of them, old and waiting,
Or because they stay indoors more.
Such dignity they have in their
Aloneness, behind those windows,
Sitting with their photographs,
Watching the days, the people pass,
Friends only with the weather.

What is it gentles their thoughts,
Makes such abandonment tolerable?
That there is something worth
Waiting for so patiently?
That now it can't be long?

CARD INDEX

for my mother

Every six months or so,
Making sure nobody's watching,
I go to the author-index in the library,
And we are there, typed on cards,
Neatly aphabetical.

WISEMAN, CHRISTOPHER STEPHEN. 1936-

(My books.
Four that I'm proud of.
Some early stuff in chapbooks)

WISEMAN, STEPHEN. 1907-1971

(His three.
When he was dying I held the hand
That wrote them, talked of the new ones
He was planning. He never read mine.
I wrote too late)

WISEMAN, TIMOTHY PETER. 1940-

(Four now. More soon.
I remember him as a baby nearly dying.
How we supported different teams.
How I used to bully him.
We're close now)

I am sad and proud here,
And as I read I think of the one
Whose name is not here, whose hopes
Were always for the three of us.
These cards will never tell it all.

I turn away, shut the drawer gently,
Leave a family pressed close together,
Whole, in perfect order.